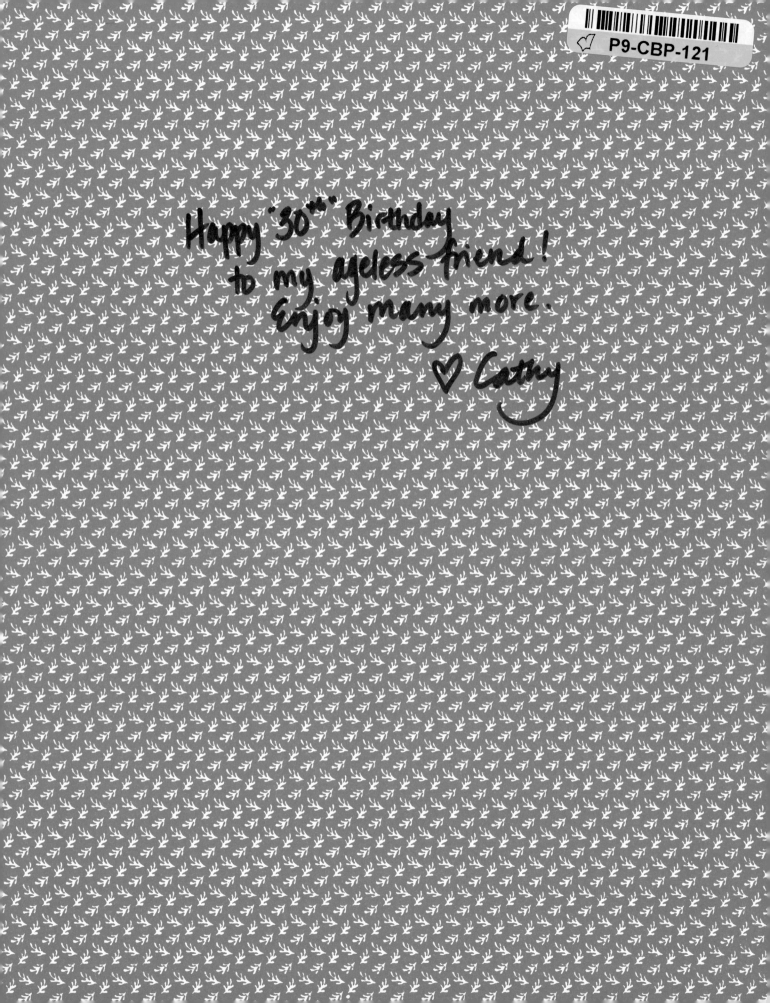

Happy "30ᵗʰ" Birthday
to my ageless friend!
Enjoy many more.
♡ Cathy

The Private World of
Tasha Tudor

The Private World of
Tasha Tudor

by Tasha Tudor
and Richard Brown

Little, Brown and Company

Boston   New York   London

FIRST EDITION

Library of Congress Cataloging-in-Publication Data

Tudor, Tasha.

    The private world of Tasha Tudor / by Tasha Tudor and Richard Brown. — 1st ed.

      p. cm.

    Includes bibliographical references.

    1. Tudor, Tasha. 2. Illustrators — United States — Biography.

ISBN 0-316-11292-5

I. Brown, Richard, 1945– . II. Title.

NC975.5.T82A2 1992

741.6′42′092 — dc20   92-8735

[B]

ACKNOWLEDGMENTS

The authors are grateful for permission to reprint illustrations from the following books:

Pages 30 and 54 from *A Time to Keep: The Tasha Tudor Book of Holidays,* written and illustrated by Tasha Tudor. Copyright © 1977 by Checkerboard Press. Reprinted with permission of Macmillan Publishing Company.

Page 30 from *Corgiville Fair,* written and illustrated by Tasha Tudor. Copyright © 1971 by Thomas V. Crowell Company. Reprinted with permission of HarperCollins Publishers.

Page 76 from *Pumpkin Moonshine,* by Tasha Tudor. Copyright © 1938 by Oxford University Press. Copyright renewed 1966 by Tasha Tudor. Reprinted by permission of Henry Z. Walck, a division of David Mckay Co., Inc.

Page 96 from *Drawn from New England,* copyright © 1979 by Bethany Tudor. Illustration by Tasha Tudor. Reprinted by permission of Philomel Books.

Pages 114 and 124 from *Tasha Tudor's Advent Calendar,* copyright © 1988 by Tasha Tudor. Reprinted by permission of Philomel Books.

12 13 14 15

IMAGO

Designed by Barbara Werden

PRINTED IN CHINA

Contents

Introduction   vii

Spring   3

Summer   33

Autumn   75

Winter   107

Selected Bibliography   131

Annotations   133

Introduction

FROM the time she was a little girl, Tasha Tudor has known exactly what she wanted: to live on a secluded farm where she could surround herself with a garden and a menagerie of household pets and barnyard animals, and to illustrate children's books. She has succeeded famously at both. Today, the much-celebrated illustrator is working on her seventy-eighth book, and lives in a setting of her own creation that reflects an unabashed admiration for the taste and lifestyle of an earlier time, hidden away in the softly rounded hills of southeastern Vermont.

I first came to know Tasha and her special world when I was asked by a magazine to photograph her garden. My daughter, I recalled, had done a report on her for a fifth-grade project, so I had some sense of what to expect as I negotiated the narrow dirt road that wound toward her home. Certainly some corgis would be in evidence, those short-legged Welsh herding dogs that have become her trademark. Her garden would be informal and lavishly planted, and the house, I suspected, would be the classic settler's Cape. I was hardly prepared, however, for what I found as woods abruptly gave way to a clearing, and Tasha's house and barns

came into view. Quite simply, I felt as if I'd driven into the past — into a magical place "east of Vermont and west of New Hampshire," caught in the year 1830, idealized yet clearly real, as the strong scent of buck goat and the drying wash that fluttered on the line in the distance attested. The weathered rambling farmhouse and outbuildings were nestled into the hillside, and softened by the vines, clinging roses, and lilacs that nearly engulfed them. A handful of floppy-eared goats grazed in the barnyard, doves strutted and preened along the roof ridge, and a brightly colored flock of chickens wandered about, squabbling and scratching in the dirt. The sharp sweet smell of woodsmoke hung in the warm air, unmistakable evidence that the owner of the house still preferred to cook with an old cast-iron kitchen range. The scene before me looked like a nineteenth-century farmscape by George Henry Durrie or Winslow Homer, or, of course, an illustration by Tasha Tudor.

My knock on the door was answered by a chorus of barking, and then Tasha appeared amidst a surging wave of corgis, her hair tied back under a kerchief, dressed in a faded ankle-length frock and calico apron, and, as I soon learned was her habit, barefoot. She was clearly amused by my ill-concealed surprise at her quaint appearance. "My friends refer to this as my gleaner's outfit," she said with a self-deprecating smile.

Inside, the house was dark and ancient looking, but bits of sunlight made their way through the leaf-shaded windows and formed intricate dancing patterns on the walls. Exotic birds chirped and trilled from a dozen ornate birdcages, and something tantalizing bubbled away in a copper pot on the back of the stove. As my eyes grew more accustomed to the dimness of the room, I felt again that unsettling yet pleasurable sensation of centuries colliding. The interior of the house looked even more like an old painting than the outside. Highlights gleamed off antique china and brass in the umber shadows, and the light had a delicious Vermeer quality. Everywhere there was something begging to be photographed, and I knew that if Tasha would agree, I had to return and record what I could of this remarkable world.

It took a determined spirit and fierce resolve for Tasha to live out her childhood dreams. She has lived by a maxim of one of her favorite writers, George Bernard Shaw. "I can't quote it exactly," she confesses, "but the idea is that so many people complain about their circumstances, but those who get ahead make their own circumstances." Tasha has certainly made hers. She was born to a strongly independent artist mother and an ingenious naval architect father, whose families had played prominent roles in Boston society for several generations. Her grandparents and parents brushed shoulders with a remarkable assortment of nineteenth- and early-twentieth-century luminaries: Emerson, the Alcotts, Thoreau, Mark Twain, Oliver Wendell Holmes, Jr., Einstein, and Buckminster Fuller, to name but a few. Her great-grandfather had been known throughout the region as "Crazy Tudor, the Ice King," a rags-to-riches phenomenon who perfected the technique of harvesting ice from New England ponds and shipping it to every corner of the globe. By the time of Tasha's childhood, however, the family had reached a state of "genteel poverty," and at the age of nine, following her parents' divorce, she led a somewhat peripatetic existence, spending winters in Redding, Connecticut, with a colorful and much-beloved "bohemian" family, and many weekends and summers with her mother wherever she might be painting, at her studio in New York City, or on Boston's Beacon Hill.

Characteristically, Tasha flourished in the loosely structured Redding environment, "running wild in the woods" and taking part in an ongoing round of charades, plays, and marionette shows with a close circle of friends and relatives. Time alone was spent making dolls, her own clothes, and "drawing from the time I can remember." Tasha still has many of the sketchbooks filled with impressions of farm animals, women in elegant long gowns, and keenly observed details from nature, and miniature one-of-a-kind children's books done while she was in her teens.

By the time of her marriage, Tasha's first published book, *Pumpkin Moonshine*, had been accepted by Oxford University Press, and she was eager to find her own place in the country. The young couple acquired a decrepit but beautiful seventeen-room farmhouse in Webster, New Hampshire. Here, Tasha continued her career in earnest and raised four children without benefit of plumbing or electricity until the youngest was five, while somehow finding the time to make the house livable, milk a cow, care for a lively collection of chickens, geese, sheep, and pigs, and tend her vegetable and flower gardens. Once again, Tasha thrived on difficulty and hard work, but her husband did not, and the couple, like her parents, eventually divorced. As a single parent, she worked with even more determination to "keep the wolf from the door," through sales of her illustrations, portrait commissions, and by performing marionette shows with the help of her two sons and daughters.

Once her family was grown, and with the proceeds from the success of *Corgiville Fair*, Tasha purchased a plot of abandoned farmland across the Connecticut River in Vermont. It had the requisite amount of privacy and a sloping southern exposure to give the gardens she envisioned a fighting chance

against the rigorous climate. Her older son, Seth, built the house and barns according to her plans and work began immediately on the walls for the gardens and the planting of flowering crab apples, pears, and apples in the orchard. Now, after twenty years of Vermont weather, the buildings have mellowed sufficiently to trick any visitor into assuming they are from another time, and the gardens have reached magnificent maturity. And Tasha, living in the surroundings she has always wanted, continues to work from dawn to dusk, gardening, milking her goats, spinning and weaving, and above all, painting.

She is without pretension about her art. There is no studio, just a small corner, "like a chipmunk's nest," in the winter kitchen where she sits beside a north-facing window, balancing her work on her lap. Paints, brushes and pens, bottles of colored inks, pastels, and sketches for current projects lie scattered in creative disarray, all within arm's reach.

But the small, finely detailed watercolors with their jewel-like colors, and intricately painted borders, are only the best-known part of Tasha's multifaceted inventiveness. There are the precisely crafted dolls and their meticulously furnished three-story house, and the dozens of marionettes made over the years, each brimming with personality and liberal touches of her humor. Also an adept weaver and spinner, Tasha patiently threads her loom with hundreds and hundreds of the finest flax threads, which she weaves into beautifully textured linen, and Sunday afternoons are always spent sewing new dresses.

Then there is Tasha the collector. Chests and closets are filled with antique clothing and accessories, early-nineteenth-century cooking utensils hang in a pleasing clutter above the stove and fireplace, and the barn is fully equipped with old wooden farming implements, Her home, however, is hardly a lifeless museum of objects from the young republic. The linsey-woolsey homespun dresses are worn when the weather gets cold, and the more elegant gowns are taken out for special occasions, or for friends to try on and to catch, perhaps, a fleeting sensation of what life in an earlier time might have been like. The everyday china is the blue-and-white Canton that once served as ballast in her great-grandfather's ice ships. "I'd rather use a thing and have it broken than hide it in a box and never see it" is her refreshingly hedonistic philosophy.

But what gives Tasha her greatest pleasure is clearly her garden. It commands her attention from April's thaw to October's killing frost, and the result is breathtaking. In mid May when pink and white crab apples stand in pools of yellow daffodils and pale lemon narcissus, or in early July when towering spikes of deep lavender, cerulean blue, and creamy white delphinium rule the extravagantly planted perennial border, it is, as she will freely boast, "Paradise on earth."

I can personally attest to Tasha's artistry as a cook. She is a virtuoso with the cast-iron stove that dominates the low-ceilinged kitchen, coaxing and cajoling, deftly adjusting flues and dampers, rattling stovelids, stoking the firebox, exhorting it to optimum performance. How many times, after a long morning of recalcitrant flash equipment or less-than-cooperative weather, has Tasha cheered me up with something mouth-watering from that old black behemoth. While the corgis snoozed at our feet, we would lunch on delectable chicken soup, golden biscuits, and tart rosé-colored applesauce served *à la* Tasha with a dollop of fresh goat's milk yogurt and a sprinkling of cookie crumbs, and tea, made the right way, with loose leaves in a warmed hundred-and-fifty-year-old teapot.

As we ate, the parrots would perform their jungle antics, recite verses from "The Owl and the Pussycat," and do uncanny imitations of Tasha answering the telephone, sneezing, blowing her nose, or scolding: "Now, dogs," or "You nasty bird!" "I've been trying to get them to say, 'You repulsive fowl!' but they just won't do it," she complained. It was during these repasts that I kept a small tape recorder running, and in between the parrot squawks, the clinking of antique china and old silver, and my appreciative lip-smacking, tried to capture the essence of Tasha's conversation. I wanted Tasha's world to be presented in her own voice. Outspoken, laced with quotations that range from Shakespeare to Walter de la Mare, tinged with a trace of nineteenth-century formality, yet filled with wit, emphatic bons mots, and humorous anthropomorphisms, her speech is a delight. The weather is "sulking." The wood stove has "crises." For Tasha, the moon is always "she" and thistles are "definitely male!" I took special pleasure in hearing tales of Tasha's childhood, her views on current fashion or the women's movement, her skirmishes with invading rodents, or the adventures of her tame Edgar Allen Crow when he traveled with Tasha to a posh New York hotel. (He snitched jewelry and slept in the bathtub.)

As is always the case with projects of this nature, much was missed. Wonderful things were said when the tape recorder wasn't running, and my mind is filled with unphotographed special moments — the ones that got away because the light was too dim or the eye was quicker than the hand. Tasha emerging from the rhododendron garden at dusk, for instance, carrying a five-foot bouquet of flower-laden branches for the house, or her extinguishing of a fiery corgi fight by adroitly scooping up one of the snarling dogs and dunking it in the rain barrel. But fortunately, with a personality as rich and vital and creative as Tasha's there was an overabundance of opportunity. Here then, as the seasons come and go, drawn from photographs, her words, and her art, is a portrait of Tasha Tudor and her uniquely beautiful, private world.

The Private World of
Tasha Tudor

Spring

I always wanted to live in Vermont, and because I always get my own way, this is where I settled. The first thing I did was plant daffodils — over a thousand. The road was impassable, so I carried them in by backpack. And my rhododendrons I brought in through a foot of snow in a wheelbarrow.

To think that Seth, my small boy who used to play with blocks, built this entire house and barn with his own hands, that's pretty nice! He did it completely alone, too, except my younger son, Tom, came and shingled the roof. Seth would recite Chaucer's *Miller's Tale* from memory, superbly, and it was marvelous to hear him as he was building. He has a fine voice and it was the unexpurgated version, of course. He relished it.

I had a friend who had an old house built in 1740 in Webster, New Hampshire, where I lived before coming here. I always loved that house and this is it, an exact copy only in reverse because of the lay of the land. First came the barn. Before it was sided it looked perfectly beautiful, like the skeleton of a ship, and it was all bright new wood. I lived in it that first summer, up until November, with all my birds in one of the goat stalls.

What you want is entirely a state of mind. I

think happiness is a state of mind. Everything here gives me satisfaction. My home, my garden, my animals, the weather, the state of Vermont.

Spring comes late here. The temperature sticks at 40° for weeks on end. But then the woodcock sings his courting song and the peepers start to trill. The goslings hatch out, and I open the dovecote and let the doves come and go.

On hot spring days, when it's very still, the white-throated sparrow sits on top of a dead tree in the swamp and sings his plaintive song. I've never heard a nightingale, but the sparrow's song is one of the most beautiful I know. His other name is the peabody bird — he says it as he sings. Later the thrushes and the veeries come and several families of bluebirds. They like my old apple trees, but they court trouble by nesting too low.

After the snow finally goes, the first thing I do is take the boughs off my lavender plants, but you have to uncover things slowly because the weather in New England, as Mark Twain said, is nine months of winter and three months of bad sledding. The other day we had 90°, there was one day in between, and the next morning there was a frost. I knew it was going to freeze when I walked down to the goatshed in the evening. When you go barefoot, you feel the chill penetrating the ground and you can tell.

MY mother and father were divorced when I was nine, and I was sent to live with close friends, Aunt Gwen and Uncle Michael and their daughter, a remarkably unconventional family in Redding, Connecticut. Mama was a very independent woman and wanted to pursue her career as an artist in New York City, which she felt was impossible with a young child in tow. Suddenly, here I was, this proper little Bostonian girl raised by a Scottish nanny, thrown into this completely unorthodox household. I won't tell you their last name because I think they'd be embarrassed, but they came from a very celebrated ancestry of early New Englanders.

In Redding we lived like bohemians on shredded wheat and tomatoes and rice, and then on the weekends Uncle Michael would come up from New York where he worked during the week and bring oranges and a box of candy and a roast of meat. They thought nothing of their things. They had their great-grandfather's Chinese export teapot all stitched to bits, and the beautiful silver spoons were just thrown into the dishpan. It was so peculiar.

They lived in one of the oldest houses in Redding, a saltbox that had a long keeping room at the back with a huge fireplace and hearth. They must have needed two yoke of oxen to bring it in. It was a large, extended family, full of aunts and uncles with numerous offspring who would congregate on holidays and put on plays and charades by candlelight. We went from holiday to holiday thinking about what we would perform. All of them were excellent actors, every single one.

They had a huge dress-up chest, a Norwegian dower chest as big as a table, brick red and decorated with flower painting and the date, seventeen something, and the initials of the bride. They dumped all the costumes in it that they thought would be good, and we used real makeup and false beards. I was just mad about anything old-fashioned, and there were some grandmother's dresses in it from the 1860s.

We had a secret society and pie-eating contests and large banquets; we had literary games and made up sinister verses and told stories late into the night. It turned out to be the best thing that ever happened to me. It changed my life.

MY education, such as it was, revolved around books. Aunt Gwen read aloud to us as only she could until ten or eleven every night, and then we went to school at eight the next morning, but it didn't seem to affect us. She read all of Scott and Dickens, Wilkie Collins, and Conan Doyle. I was conversant with *Huckleberry Finn* and *The Mysterious Stranger* from the age of seven.

Of course we were brought up on Beatrix Potter, and I loved *The Wind in the Willows*. That was one of my father's favorite books. Walt Disney should be sued for cheapening it as he did. Imagine it, Mickey Mousing all those nice characters. I'm surprised he didn't do it with the New Testament.

There are certain books that you enjoy as a child, but when you read them again as an adult you find there's nothing to them. But then there are others that you get just as much pleasure out of: *Gulliver's Travels*, *The Wonderful Adventures of Nils*, *Robinson Crusoe*, and especially *Moby-Dick*. That book has been ruined by teachers! The pictures it creates in your mind you never forget. You can even smell the food of the inn in the opening chapter. When I read a story, I see it like a movie, moving and all in color. Books are very real to me. I greatly admire Emily Dickinson, who said, "There is no Frigate like a Book / To take us Lands away."

What flowers should have above all else is fragrance. My camelias would be the perfect flower if only they had the fragrance of a gardenia. Their petals look as if they were made of porcelain, but they have no scent.

I'M drawn to the old ways, convinced that I lived before, in the 1830s. Everything comes so easily to me from that period, of that time: threading a loom, growing flax, spinning, milking a cow. Einstein said that time is like a river, it flows in bends. If we could only step back around the turns, we could travel in either direction. I'm sure it's possible. When I die, I'm going right back to 1830.

I T'S exciting to see things coming up again, plants that you've had twenty or thirty years. It's like seeing an old friend. You rejoice that the foxgloves haven't been killed, and lament over vole damage and things of that sort. I feed the voles Ex-Lax, which does them in pretty well.

On the south side of the house, where a hill cuts the cold north wind, the winter aconite, that little yellow buttercup, is the first thing to appear, followed by the snowdrops and pussy willows. Then the daffodils and crab apples start to open.

Daffodils are an optimistic flower, and foolproof. You know what Shakespeare said: "Daffodils, / That come before the swallow dares, and take / The winds of March with beauty." They say you should throw the bulbs on the ground and then plant them where they fall. But I've never done that, and I never use a bulb planter. Those are the most ridiculous things! They sell them to ladies in garden catalogues and you're supposed to dig one little hole at a time. I plant them in big clumps with a trusty shovel. I make several large holes all around and put quite a few in. That's why it makes such a spectacular look when they bloom.

WHAT really got me thinking about illustrating children's books was I discovered Hugh Thompson's illustrations for *The Vicar of Wakefield* in my mother's library and I looked at it and said, "That's what I'm going to do." I'd drawn from the time I could remember, and of course my mother was a painter. Her picture of my brother reading hangs in an honored spot in the winter kitchen and is much admired by all my guests — and my parrots.

Everyone who likes my illustrations says, "Oh, you must be so enthralled with your creativity." That's nonsense. I'm a commercial artist, and I've done my books because I needed to earn my living, to keep the wolf away from the door, and to buy more bulbs!

I didn't come from a family of wealth. They had reached a state of genteel poverty, let us say. But they knew everyone who was worth knowing in Boston society: Mrs. Gardner, Abigail Adams, Maxfield Parrish, and John Singer Sargent — he did a charcoal sketch of my brother. Mark Twain was a great friend of Papa's. But don't embarrass me, it's not good taste to boast.

It was a very tightly knit group. So many of these people had been friends for generations. I especially remember Justice Davis, a prominent Boston judge who used to come visit and bounce me on his knee and go, "Trot, trot to Boston, Trot, trot to Lynn." He wore buttoned leather boots and he always had peppermints in his pocket.

I've always liked justices. I adored Oliver Wendell Holmes, Jr., who lived just down the road from us. I used to sit in his lap. He had a large gold watch, a repeater, which he would take out of his pocket — you know how smooth old gold feels, and it would be warm and I'd hold it in my hand. Oh, I just loved him! He had white hair and a big handlebar mustache, and he always wore a black suit and his watch chain. I was fascinated because he still had bullets in him from the Civil War. They never came out.

I was very insecure as a girl, though I'm quite bold now. I was different, teased in school because I was so connected with the past, wore old-fashioned dresses, and wouldn't cut my hair. My mother and brother were very disappointed that I didn't care for the things they felt were important, like the Junior League and the Vincent Club, being a debutante and coming out in Boston society. I didn't give a darn about that. I only wanted to work in my garden and milk my cow.

THE big spring event of my childhood always occurred on the first warm day when we walked five miles to the country store and were allowed to buy a five-cent chocolate bar and all sorts of frightful things. We shed our boots and the long winter underwear that went to our ankles, and we felt like sylphs with the winged feet of Perseus.

When I'm working in the barn or house I often think of all the errors I've made in my life. But then I quickly put that behind me and think of water lilies. They will always eradicate unpleasant thoughts. Or goslings are equally comforting in their own way.

Have you ever noticed a gosling's face? The little buttonhole stitch around the eyes, and the way their down goes just so. Oh, they're exquisite! And their little dark beaks, and the tiny little scales on their perfectly formed feet. I think they're the most enchanting of all the young — other than goat kids and small corgis.

Have you ever brought up goslings in a box by the kitchen stove? Don't you love the noise they make, that funny little whistling trill when they're content. It's such a delicious noise, sort of a reedy twitter. Oh, it's very soothing.

IN June every possible hour is spent tending the garden. But it gives me such satisfaction. I haven't any modesty when it comes to my garden. I'll boast like mad.

I'm very familiar with all these plants and knew they'd be pretty combined: yellow Louisiana iris, and lupines, sweet rocket, and oriental poppies. Usually they're a bright vermilion, but this is the pale pink one I'm very fond of. I've always had a clear picture of how I wanted my garden to look. In a nursery they say, "Can we help you?" No! I know just what I want — or don't want. African violets, for example. They're loathsome. It's their velvet look. I'm a frightful show-off when it comes to my garden. It's Paradise on earth!

I'VE always done borders of sticks or ribbons or flowers around my illustrations and I don't even know why I decided to. I don't even remember when I didn't. People like to find things in them.

Another appeal of my drawings, I think, is that they are done from actuality, not imagined. I know which side a cow is milked from, and what side you should mount a horse from, and how to make a haystack. It's not made up. The people in my pictures are my own grandchildren and friends, and the surroundings are drawn from my surroundings. The flowers are growing wild in my fields or are from my garden. People who come to visit say, "Oh, it's like walking into one of your illustrations."

Summer

THERE is no other dog that can compare to a corgi. They're the epitome of beauty. Apollo can't hold a candle to my Owyn. He has royal blood, the same sire as Queen Elizabeth's corgis, that's why I named him Owyn Tudor after my ancestors. Corgis are Welsh in origin and there are two kinds: Cardigans, which are heavy-headed and have tails that go all the way down, and Pembrokes, like mine, that have no tails and are more refined.

My very first corgi was bought by my son Tom for ten guineas from a Reverend Mr. Jones, a vicar in Pembrokeshire, who shipped him over in a tea chest. It was love at first sight and I was determined I had to have more. I've had up to thirteen or fourteen at one time, which causes a lot of commotion underfoot, especially when people come to call.

They're such characters — a mixture of a dog and a cat, I think. They especially don't like to be scolded in public. They talk back; they growl and show their teeth and pretend they're frightfully savage. However, they never criticize. You're always beautiful to them.

I take great pains in feeding them the best. Never canned dog food, I wouldn't dream of it!

They always have fresh homemade soup, or goat's meat, and lots of garlic. That's why they don't have fleas.

How could you resist a corgi? Look at their faces. I find them thoroughly adorable, particularly when they're little. And in the winter it's very cozy to sleep with a nice warm corgi in the small of your back to cut the drafts. We always had a medley of doggies when the children were growing up — collies, wolfhounds, terriers, and then corgis above all. I find them irresistible. They are my trademark.

I started putting corgis in my artwork as soon as I got my first puppy. The minute I saw him I was done for.

Of course, *Corgiville Fair*, of all my books, is my most favorite. My land in Vermont was bought with the money I earned from it. It's the one book I've kept all intact — all the sketches and colored originals. They stayed out in the woodshed in an old bureau drawer for three years before I did anything with them. I never thought people would be interested.

It was really done for my children. I used to make up stories for them about a place called Corgiville, that was "west of New Hampshire and east of Vermont." The boggarts, those spotted mischief-makers, are based on a Scandinavian troll doll that a Swedish fan gave to me, and Seth just lost his heart to him. Boggarts are very interested in plumbing and things like that. They're very naughty and risqué, and their arms come off so they can go down pipes very readily and cause inconveniences. I think some of my public were rather jolted. They wanted sweet little girls. Little do they know the real artist!

MY family originally came from Boston, hub of the universe, and I'm very proud of being a Yankee. I have a frightful New England conscience. I would never dream of leaving a bill unpaid. And you don't break your word when you make a promise. If you say you'll do something, you've got to do it. Nor do you lie. Sometimes, however, to get out of unpleasant visits and such, you can handle the truth lightly. Goats are the most useful things when you get bored with a party. You can say you have to get home to do the milking. It's like having a Bunbury. Have you never had a Bunbury? He's an imaginary friend or invalid that you have to go and attend if you want to get away.

Are you not trained to be a hypocrite from the cradle up? To tell white lies and not to be rude to people when you feel quite differently. You can't be completely outspoken, can you. There's that wonderful story about J. P. Morgan calling a young man to task for committing some indiscretion. The young man said, "Well, at least I did it out in the open, I didn't do it behind closed doors,"

and Mr. Morgan turned to him and said, "Young man, that's what closed doors are for!"

You have to pretend an awful lot, thank people for something you don't like, say you're glad to see someone when really you wish they were in Australia. When I'm alone I can be completely myself. I can tell the cat what's on my mind, and when they're recalcitrant, I can tell the goats exactly what I think of them and no one can hear me.

I enjoy solitude. It's probably selfish, but why bother about it. Life is much too important, as Oscar Wilde said, to be taken seriously. I feel so sorry for those mothers who are devastated by loneliness when their children fly the coop and don't want to live at home anymore. They feel lost, but look what exciting things can be done. Life isn't long enough to do all you could accomplish. And what a privilege even to be alive. In spite of all the pollutions and horrors, how beautiful this world is. Supposing you only saw the stars once every year. Think what you would think. The wonder of it!

BECAUSE I gardened as a little girl, and my mother and grandmother were passionate gardeners before me, I grew up with flowers, knew them by their look and feel, and called them by all their old colloquial names. Dame's rocket, sweet William, monkshood, and meadow rue — the old-fashioned names are so much prettier. Delphinium were always called larkspur. *Clematis autumnale* was virgin's bower. The sound of "foxglove" is so much pleasanter than "digitalis."

GARDENING has untold rewards. You never have to go on a diet. At age seventy-six I can still wear my wedding dress and still chin myself. I've never been depressed in my whole life and I've never had a headache. They must be awful. I attribute it to goat's milk and gardening.

I raise all my own fruits and vegetables, put up my own carrots and turnips and beets. I try to be self-sufficient.

Midsummer is the time for berries: raspberries, blueberries, thimbleberries — they're very dark and shiny. Have you ever tasted them? They make the most delicious jam. But best of all are the strawberries. There's nothing like the taste of just-picked strawberries to my mind. I try and grow the most delicate varities. You would have to say they're ambrosia, especially when they're still warmed from the sun. And you should taste my strawberry ice cream made with fresh goat's cream!

A girlhood friend who later died in childbirth used to keep a flock of white doves in her garden, and they would flutter down and sit on her shoulders when she fed them. I've always kept that picture in my memory. I like beautiful things around me and I think doves are very beautiful — but very stupid. To defend themselves they just blow themselves up and strut around.

My fantails are not very strong fliers and hawks are very fond of them. I did have white kings that could really fly well, and they'd tumble like a raven. They would ride high on the air currents and then fall over and over and over all the way down to the ground.

D ON'T you think lettuce poppies are stunning? They look especially well when there are great masses of them. The foliage has that gray-green color of pale lettuce. These come from my grandmother's garden and I've carried the seeds with me everywhere. The lavender ones go to only my best and choicest friends. I sow all the poppy varieties I can: Shirley poppies, and Welsh poppies, and poppies from Flanders fields.

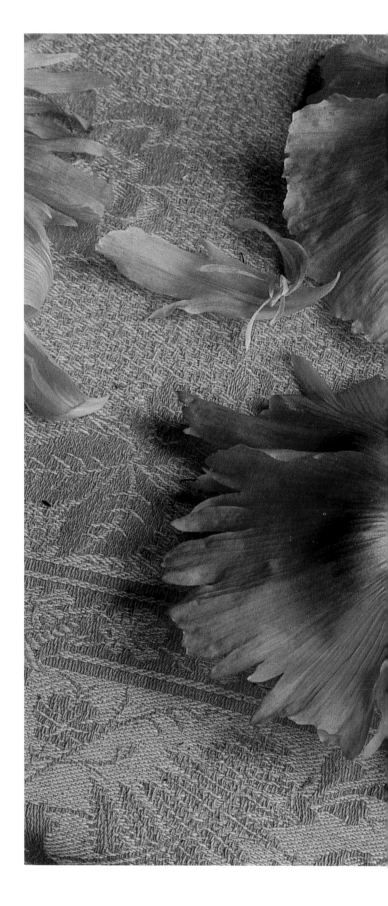

LIKE Pygmalion and Galatea, I made a doll and then I fell in love with her. And I feel rather guilty because I'm much more attached to her than any of the family dolls that I've had for years. Her name is Emma, and her suitor, who was made some time ago, is Captain Thaddeus Crane.

I remember the amazing discovery, at age seven or eight, when suddenly I realized that I didn't have to talk out loud with my dolls. I could think everything in my head. That was a big revelation to me. I could play anything I wanted secretly, and I didn't have to say it. Because I was the youngest, I was very much an alone child. Really, you are always alone with your own mind.

WHEN I lived in New Hampshire and my children were still in school, we put on marionette shows in the neighboring towns to earn extra spending money. One of our most popular was *Jack and the Beanstock* because you could see the beanstock growing and the ogre was very impressive. Another one of our productions was *Little Red Riding Hood;* the smaller children in the audience would usually cry when Granny was devoured by the wolf, so we thought that was quite effective. Actually, she fell behind the bed.

For *Saint George and the Dragon*, Seth, who was only ten, concocted a splendid beast. It was constructed of heavy silver paper, all in sections, so it undulated properly. We made a silk tongue and a big pouch in the dragon's mouth, which we filled with ground-up charcoal, and ran a long tube from an old enema bag through him. Tom would lie under the stage and at the right moment, when the dragon was about to fight Saint George, he would blow on the tube and these great clouds of black smoke and this red flickering tongue would emerge. Oh, he was a dandy! And for *The Knights of the Round Table* we made two large wooden horses and had a big jousting tourney in the middle of the stage with the knights in full armor, and a great clashing of tin pans out in back. It was superb.

When I built my home in Vermont, I just had to have a marionette theater, so we converted what was going to be a shed for my buck goats into one. Seth built rows of benches and a stage with two bridges over it so there would be room for some of the grandchildren to operate characters as well. The bridge is what you stand on and lean over to work the marionettes. That's why they have such long strings. One evening, every summer, we invite all our friends to a lavish production with sound effects and music, and an intermission and refreshments. It's very professional.

I've always loved the theater. And you can get effects with marionettes that you can't get with humans. I'm longing to make an Ichabod Crane. I'm still hoping I live long enough to do *The Legend of Sleepy Hollow.*

THACKERAY'S *Rose and the Ring* was our most ambitious production. It's made for a marionette show. There are three villains and two heroines and several heroes. It just outdoes everything. We made over forty marionettes for that one play. You can't change a marionette's costume, so we had to make three different Countess Gruffanuffs. We worked on it for over a year.

I also have a marionette eight-piece corgi orchestra. They're masters at playing Vivaldi. And our guest conductor is a cat, Pasquale Fellini, who uses his tail for a baton when he gets overexcited.

SOME people call this a cottage garden, but it's just a good messy garden. There's no plan. It's not like painting — I just stick the plants in. I like large quantities of blooms all jumbled together: Reine de Violette roses, thalictrum, artemisia, iris, pinks, clematis, peonies, and forget-me-nots. I like flowers in real abundance. If you have just so much money, spend it all on one variety and make a big splash.

My garden is built in levels with lots of stone walls. The snakes think my walls are Ritz-Carltons.

There's a lovely tame one, which lives in the largest wall just before the house. He was injured when he was tiny. I brought him inside and made a nest of moss and raised him up until he was a foot long. Then I had to let him go because he was getting too big. He would sit curled up in my hand at night while I read in bed. Snakes love warmth, and he would make a perfect circle on my palm. Have you ever studied a snake's face? — how optimistic they look. They have an eternal smile. I think they're laughing at man's folly.

PEONIES have an intoxicating smell, and they're so soft and creamy looking. I like the pale pink ones best, but there's a whiteish-yellow one called Prairie Moon that's magical. Their foliage remains beautiful all summer. They die nicely, in other words; not like some roses that die like old dishrags.

JUST for fun, my family invented a religion like the Shakers we called Stillwater. I'm eldress, and we have a big celebration on Midsummer's Eve. It's really a state of mind. Stillwater connotes something very peaceful, you see, life without stress. Nowadays, people are so jeezled up. If they took some chamomile tea and spent more time rocking on the porch in the evening listening to the liquid song of the hermit thrush, they might enjoy life more.

It all started because we knew the Shakers at Canterbury Village, New Hampshire, when we lived nearby. They used to come and have tea and we'd exchange cuttings. I loved their frocks and things, and I was especially fond of one of them, Sister Alice, who kept bees. We really invented our Stillwater belief so we could have a party out in the barn on Midsummer's Eve. It didn't amount to much religion except for a good dance and lots of delicious things to eat.

Stillwater believers are very hedonistic. Life is to be enjoyed, not saddled with. Do you know that lovely quotation from Fra Giovanni? He was an old monk from away back who wrote to his patron, "The gloom of the world is but a shadow; behind it, yet within our reach is joy. Take joy." That's the first commandment of the Stillwater religion. Joy is there for the taking. Some people are born pessimists and some are born optimists. I'm definitely an optimist.

WHY do women want to dress like men when they're fortunate enough to be women? Why lose our femininity, which is one of our greatest charms? We get much more accomplished by being charming than we would by flaunting around in pants and smoking. I'm very fond of men. I think they're wonderful creatures. I love them dearly. But I don't want to look like one.

When women gave up their long skirts, they made a grave error. Things half seen are so much more mysterious and delightful. Remember the term "a neatly turned ankle"? Think of the thrill that gentlemen used to get if they caught even a glimpse of one. Now women go around in their union suits. And what a multitude of sins you could cover up with a long skirt if you had piano legs.

MY antique clothing collection is a great folly of mine. The majority are from the 1830s, but I have examples from every style and decade from 1770 to 1870. It's very common for a friend who tries on one of my old dresses to feel transported to another time. It gives a different perspective on life.

I myself feel much more at home in an old frock. There's no feeling of dressing up; they just feel right! I've collected everything: stays, corsets, bustles, hoops, parasols, gloves, wristers, muffs, bonnets, and even an Empire "barnyard cape" made of peacock and pheasant feathers, which was all the rage when Jefferson was president.

THE lilies bloom in August and the Michaelmas daisies, and the annuals are trying to outdo themselves before they're laid low — the zinnias, petunias, pot marigolds, and nasturtiums. They all seem to become more brilliant then. And the grass in the meadows becomes so emerald green.

You're just hoping there isn't a frost the first week in September. It kills all the flowers and then you have wonderful Indian summer for two months and your garden is gone. It doesn't seem quite right. I'm sure in Paradise it's not arranged that way.

I used to dread the end of summer. As soon as the goldenrod bloomed it meant I had to go back to school. I hated it! But it's a beautiful time of the year when the southwest wind blows with a distinctive sweet scent and the crickets' chirping starts to slow down and the constellations shift in the night sky. Spring's chicks and ducklings have grown into fine plump specimens and the geese gather under the apple trees looking for the first ripe apples to drop.

Autumn

❧❧❧❧❧

I
N the fall there are the vegetables to harvest
from the garden: pumpkins, potatoes, carrots, and usually a splendid crop of onions.
They like soil with good tilth and wood ashes,
which I have in great quantity. After I pull all the
onions up, I let them dry and then braid them and
hang them up.

At midday the September sun is lower in the
sky and there's a lovely light that slants into the
house and makes dramatic birdcage shadows
across the wall.

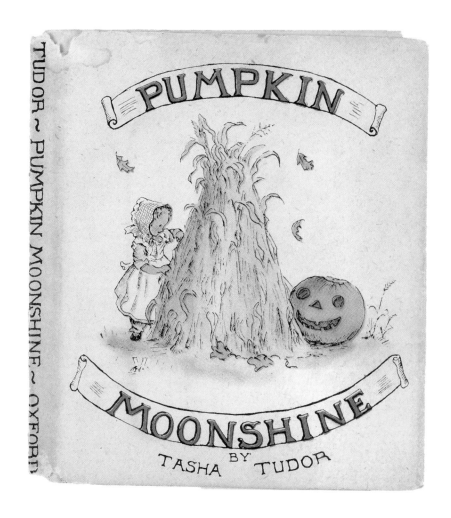

Pumpkin Moonshine was my first book, done in 1938. I went to every publisher in New York, I think, and finally Oxford University Press accepted it. I was just married and the child I drew in that book, people said, looked exactly like the children I eventually had, so I guess it was wishful thinking. My first royalty check was seventy-five dollars. I thought I'd made a mint!

W ORKING in the garden in autumn is delightful, with the clean smell of frost-bitten ferns and witch hazel in the air and no insects to bother about. There are always great numbers of bulbs to be put in the ground — over two thousand this fall, counting the lilies.

The other day I heard the first Canada geese go over as I was planting. Their calls give me such a primordial feeling. And to see a flock of snow geese flying over the white birch trees by the mailbox on a fair day is a sight to take the breath away.

THERE is a mystery pear tree growing in my orchard. I dug it up and brought it with me from Webster, New Hampshire, when I moved. It was quite full grown and wasn't happy. It never attained the beautiful shape here that it had previously. We always called it "the pretty pear tree," but I've never known what variety it is. It's not a Clapp Favorite, and I don't think it's any kind of Bartlett, and it's not a Beurre Bosc. Every fall it's laden with fruit and I bottle some. They taste so much better than boughten ones. He who plants pears, plants for his heirs.

I love the feel of feathers. My parrot Hannah is lovely to touch, and if you bury your nose in her feathers it's delicious. Every night I let her out and she washes the dishes with me and oversees the cooking of supper and talks to me. Occasionally she bites my ear and I give her my opinion of her and put her back in her cage. She knows she's not supposed to, but sometimes she can't resist.

Parrots nibble and say naughty things. You have to chaperone them constantly. They get into mischief. I have friends whose parrot escaped from her perch while they were out and ate the leg off their rosewood piano.

WHEN I was a child we cherished our toys, because we couldn't get another if one of them broke. I was very fond of my little iron oxcart, painted yellow, and a toy cow on wheels, and I was frightfully cross when my Scottish nanny took her horns off for fear I'd pierce myself.

The last time I counted the caged birds, I had forty-one: a society finch, a cinnamon finch, Nunn finches, and lots of zebra finches, the canaries, a cockatiel, the little African diamond doves, Chinese nightingales, and of course Pegler and Hannah, my African gray parrots.

DEER-FOOTED mice make wonderful pets. They're so beguiling, with their large eyes, tiny feet, lovely tickly whiskers, and that funny shaped bottom. They stalk a bug like a cat, crawling along on their bellies. And when they stop to preen themselves, they take their tails in both hands and run their little fingers up and down to straighten the fur.

My cat used to bring them in to show off her prowess as a huntress. She wouldn't kill them and they'd be in a swoon and I'd keep them for a while and they'd recover. For three or four years I kept a pair. They raised a family and I did a whole book of sketches to illustrate Robert Burns's poem about "the best laid schemes o' mice and men / Gang aft a-gley."

THE past wasn't as romantic as people seem to think. There were many hardships, especially for women. They usually had large families of six or eight; they were pregnant most of the time or nursing when they weren't. Think of all the spinning and knitting and sewing and cooking and woodgathering. It was constant. No wonder that saying, "Man may work from sun to sun, / But woman's work is never done."

I don't say they were unhappy, but I think they were tired most of the time. I was tired most of my younger life, with no electricity until my youngest child was five, hauling water with a shoulder yoke, and heating irons on the woodstove. But I didn't know anything different, so it didn't seem like a hardship to me.

THE original settlers of this area were planting things and making things for future generations. They thought of their children and the future and tried to make it bright. Look how they would plant whole avenues of maples for posterity.

They took pride in their work. Think of the beautiful furniture they made and their beautiful houses and the pains they took with them. And the walls they built, especially along the road, to keep the animals from straying. This land was all cleared for sheep grazing, and it was terribly rocky. So they built walls to last, out of stone.

THERE'S something wonderfully primitive about a canoe, like the sound of loons calling. It stirs something from long, long ago — another life you might have lived.

My canoe was made by Henri Vallencourt of Greenfield, New Hampshire. He's a real master of his craft. There was a long article about him in *The New Yorker*. He searches the woods for just the right size birch tree and makes his canoes entirely with a Hudson's Bay knife.

It looks big and heavy, and people look at me askance when I say I can carry it alone, but it's as light as a basket. It's amazing to think you're only floating on birchbark.

In the 1830s a lot of Americans had an inferiority complex about being such a young country. They thought Europe was better, and I couldn't agree with them less. Look what was handed to them. Imagine being given this virgin country; how beautiful it must have been. Think of the great noble trees without underbrush, the pure streams and lakes. But then we deforested the country so. The trees were the enemies of the people, and the air was constantly full of smoke from burning the immense roots and trunks to clear the land. As a people we haven't appreciated what we were given. I think Thomas Jefferson would turn in his grave if he could see what has happened, and Andrew Jackson would let out a good cuss.

CANDLES are flattering to an old face. I've always used them, and kerosene lamps. However, you have to watch that there's no draft to blow a curtain into a candle, and warn children not to lean over them. I was as nervous as a cat when my children had visitors, because it's very easy to set your hair alight. Boswell mentions how old Samuel Johnson, who was absentminded and nearsighted, was constantly scorching his wig.

Everyone says my house is dark, but people don't realize how dark old houses were. I love it dark. It's like a nice chipmunk's nest.

As a child, it was a great thrill to go out into the cornfield and pick the best pumpkins from amongst the corn stooks for jack-o'-lanterns. We called them pumpkin moonshines, because they looked like the face of the moon — especially late autumn's hunter's moon, which seems so large and orange looking.

We made a lot of Halloween. Ghosts were supposed to leave their graves and float about and frighten people. But I don't mind ghosts. They're very friendly and delightful things like mists rising out of fields. The most ghostly looking thing I've seen was a moon rainbow. Only once in my life, late in the fall. It was very pallid and phantomlike.

PEOPLE have a rose-colored lens when they look at me. They don't realize I'm human. They don't see the real me. As Mark Twain said, we are like the moon, we all have our dark side that we never show to anybody.

WHEN the nights get long and cold, the cat stays inside and sleeps in an old redware bowl. I keep her for the mice and chipmunks, which I don't like to have in too much abundance, but she's afraid of rats, only having one eye.

Cats are more troublesome than dogs to bring up. They really get into things — break china and chase birds — which corgis don't do. They eat more, and they're fussier! Did you ever read Kipling's *Just So Stories* about the cat that walked by himself? He was just the epitome of catdom, very aloof, very particular, like some people.

LAST night, I finally got the rat that's been in my kitchen. I can't get over the effrontery of his coming in here with a cat in the house, and climbing up on the table and eating apples and pears. I'd love to know how that beast got in here. If you see one, you've got fifty, I'm sure. I used to get them with a .22 rifle, but now I just don't bother. I was known as the Annie Oakley of Redding, but I can't see that well anymore.

He'd been stealing butter. I suspected kitty for a while and then I figured, no, those tooth marks were not cat marks and she wouldn't eat pears and apples, so I hid everything and set about my ruse. I've discovered that if you put the trap out three nights in a row with luscious bait on it — cheese with bacon fat and raisins — but unset, he becomes careless like any other creature. Then you set it on the fourth night and you've got him! I once caught nineteen mice on one raisin. One after the other. That was some raisin. This was a big wood rat, larger than a Norway rat, brownish with a little white on his belly and long snaggly yellow teeth, like Mr. Samuel Whiskers. I threw him in the fire and cremated him!

I've used these dishes all my life. I'd rather use a thing and have it broken than hide it in a box and never see it. That's why I wear my old 1830s frocks; most costume collectors would turn white with horror. But why have something and not enjoy it? Life is too short not to be enjoyed thoroughly.

The reason I have these things, however, is that I've taken care of them and my family before me took care of them. My Scottish nanny was very particular with the china. She always laid a couple of dish towels in the bottom of the sink — an old copper sink that made a lovely thudding sound when it was filled with water — and then she'd wash the china in that. Think of the people who have eaten from these plates, all the literati of Boston: the Alcotts, Thoreau, Daniel Webster — my grandmother was a great friend of Carey Webster — and Mr. Emerson, whom my mother remembered seeing as an old man with a sharp nose and long sideburns.

I enjoy doing housework, ironing, washing, cooking, dishwashing. Whenever I get one of those questionaires and they ask what is your profession, I always put down housewife. It's an admirable profession, why apologize for it. You aren't stupid because you're a housewife. When you're stirring the jam you can read Shakespeare.

T HERE'S an old English saying, "No fruits, no flowers, no leaves, no birds, November!" It's a time of the year when you don't have the urgency of the plants and the garden. A time for moving indoors to enjoy home and hearth. All my friends get knitting and quilting urges in November. It's a time to enjoy the pleasures of a fire and a cup of tea. I will quote Henry James from *The Portrait of a Lady:* "There are few moments in life more enjoyable than the hour set aside for the ceremony known as afternoon tea."

Winter

I don't shovel snow. It's a waste of time. I just walk through it and make a path. I keep a pair of snowshoes stuck in the snow by the back door for when it really drifts, but when I wear them the dogs have the most awful habit of fooling around right behind me and stepping on the backs of them, which is quite upsetting in both senses of the word.

You should see my corgis at sunset in the snow. It's their finest hour. About five o'clock they glow like copper. Then they come in and lie in front of the fire like a string of sausages.

The first snow is so exciting. The more the better. It puts me in mind of Christmas and all the nice things that can be done in the winter. You can hibernate without guilt in your New England conscience.

I can always smell the first storm before it comes. There's the scent of snowflakes in the air that's unmistakable. To me it's joyous. I welcome snow and winter in spite of frozen buckets and the constant hauling of wood for the fire. The first snowfall is often particularly stunning because the branches aren't frozen yet and it sticks better. I especially love it when the storm comes quietly

during the night and I wake up to a changed world. I can tell instantly. The light in my bedroom is so different when there's snow outside.

Snow on the landscape is so pleasing to paint, too. It's much easier than foliage. You don't need all those endless shades of green to give the effect. It's just white with blue shadows. And it simplifies everything. The shapes of the grasses and the weeds and the elms stand out more. They always look like lovely bouquets, elm trees do. From a distance they look as if you could pick them up by the stem.

After it's snowed, you watch for tracks. I found some of the most minute mouse tracks this morning, like little necklaces in the snow, and I could see where the rabbits had been nibbling. But the birds made the most beautiful tracks; they looked like lace.

When I was growing up in Redding, we wandered all over the countryside with our sleds. We were always sledding, and it snowed more then. You couldn't go through deep snow unless there was a crust. That made the very best sliding. There was this marvelously steep hill we used, with a pond at the bottom. Sometimes we'd get these huge cakes of ice from it and carry them to the top and then we'd spin down on them around and around. They were a real chore to push back up when you were still dizzy. And once we made an igloo and slept in it until it melted.

IT satisfies me to spin and knit and weave. I love to be self-sufficient, to learn how to make everything I use. In Webster, I grew my own wool as well, and kept six ewes and a magnificent ram we named Wully who had great curling horns and a very deep and manly voice. But I had to get rid of them because they were so foolish. They were addicted to lying in the middle of the road.

I feel at home with a spinning wheel. It's very soothing, the whirr of it; it's like a cat purring. Mine has been in the Tudor family since seventeen something, and the treadle is all worn down and smooth. Don't you love the feeling of old wood? It's so soft on the hand, warm, not cold like steel. The wheel and some of my weaving shuttles and bodkins are delightful to touch. They're just like satin, they've been used so.

When you hold a piece of hand-woven cloth,

think of how every inch of thread has passed through the fingers of the person who made it. I just finished threading my loom to weave some linen cloth and it took one thousand seven hundred and thirty-two threads! But anything worthwhile takes time. I do an hour a day. It's the best way to get this sort of thing done, little by little.

You run into trouble with looms and cats. They love to sleep on the woven cloth and they make a hammock of it. And the worst thing for spinning wheels is grandchildren.

When my own children were young and it really snowed, we had a holiday. We had telephones then that you had to crank, and they'd call and say that school was off. That was dandy! A real celebration. But we always thought of plenty of excuses to stay home when school wasn't called off. Especially when it was skating weather. Our place was just above the Blackwater River, and at certain times of the winter it would freeze, and it would be perfect to skate down. Oh, it was the most enchanting time because you had the constant change of scenery and there would be spots of clear ice. You could lie on your stomach and look down and see the fish underneath. Oh, it was wonderful! We used to take picnics and have a bonfire and make tea. It was so much better than sitting in a classroom.

They have wonderfully long winters in Corgiville. They put up a big Christmas tree and there's a lot of sleigh riding and skating on the pond out in front of the church. All the inhabitants are busy marketing and gossiping and enjoying the sports of winter. Edgar Tomcat likes to howl Christmas carols, and they have bonfires and all sorts of enjoyable doings.

THE dolls' Christmas party was held on Christmas Eve. We would have a real miniature tree, which we found in the woods and decorated, and the children all received presents from the dolls. The gifts were human sized, so they had to be piled outside the dollhouse. We tried to make all our presents — knitted things, small decorated paper boxes, little carved wooden families of mother goose and four young ones, and we would take hollowed-out walnut shells and make a hinge and set tiny birds and nests and eggs inside.

Dividing the presents between the dolls' Christmas and our Christmas made it much more peaceful. There wasn't so much confusion, and the children had all of Christmas Day to play with the toys that they got from the dolls while I was working on the tree and cooking Christmas dinner.

THE dolls were very real to my family. They went on outings with us, and the children sent them tiny letters by "Sparrow Post," and they got letters back. I wrote them, of course, but it's no different from Santa Claus. There was a constant story of their lives going on.

There is something about a dollhouse-sized world that appeals to me tremendously, and to a lot of people. It's the perfection in miniature, I think, like an acorn. A large department store in Boston had me decorate a window at Christmastime with the dolls and there were crowds of people five or six deep looking at it.

LIKE most farms in the olden part of New England my barn is attached to the house for convenience so you don't have to wade out in deep snow. Insurance men don't like it. They claim there's more fire damage, and charge more, but they're crooks. I relish the feeling, when it's really snowing out, of going to the barn to milk the goats without even having to put my boots on, but by the time I'm finished I'm also thinking how nice it will be to get back to the house and have my tea in the rocking chair with a warm corgi on the lap.

I like the smell of the barn in winter and the sound of my beasties moving around, my goats and hens and doves. They never fail to greet me in the morning very pleasantly. Right now the hens are on strike. They don't lay much during the winter, but I don't blame them, sitting on a cold nest.

Sometimes when I've been throwing hay around, it smells like summer in the barn, and the sun comes through the windows and the cracks in the boards and makes shafts of light in the dusty air. But I never long for summer in winter. What is that lovely quote from Shakespeare — "At Christmas I no more desire a rose / Than wish a snow in May's newfangled mirth." That's the idea. For everything there is a season.

CHRISTMAS has always been my family's favorite celebration. We go from Christmas to Christmas getting ready for it. I keep a huge wooden chest, and we fill it with decorations and presents over the summer and fall. I make garlands of laurel over the front door and the hen-pantry door and across the top of the fireplace. It grows wild here, but we don't have holly — it's too cold for it to set berries.

Usually we put swags of hemlock in the barn and we always give the animals something special. The goats like to have some baked goods, buns and things of that sort, and the chickens get a fitting gift of leftover stuffing from preparing the turkey. We give all the animals a Christmas tree of their own. The goats eat theirs; they love it. The parrots eat theirs, too. And the dogs get sardines in their stockings, a tin apiece. And pussy gets a catnip mouse and goes on a decided trip. Of course it's a known fact that all the animals talk on Christmas Eve.

I think the most enchanting thing we've ever done at Christmastime is the crèche in the woods. There's a path through the trees that leads across a brook to a huge ledge. In old paintings they often depict the crèche as being a sort of cave, and where the ledge overhangs, I put up forked sticks and then other sticks leaning against the rock, and I make a little manger there with all the Nativity figures and the animals in it made out of scraps of wood and pieces of old material. I take real trouble with them; the goat has an udder and everything.

We stick candles in the snow every three feet or so along the path and around the crèche. To see this winding trail of flickering candlelight leading through the pines and beeches and hemlocks, and the stars overhead, oh, it's absolutely magical! It's best with a soft, still snow. It means more to young children than the Christmas tree and all the presents. My granddaughter first saw it for her two-year-old Christmas and spoke of "the baby in the woods" for years after.

WE never put the big tree up until Christmas Eve because we light it with real candles and it's very hard to burn a fresh tree. It's always cut right from the woods. I've never used a boughten one. They're much too dry.

I've never bought a decoration either. All the ornaments are from my great-grandmother's collection and date from 1850: round and pear-shaped ones, and beautiful bunches of grapes made of colored glass painted with mercury inside to give them that silvery look. The red are the most desirable and the rarest. I'm very lucky to have a collection that's never been broken up. There are also the most wonderful icicles, and the candle holders, instead of being clip-on affairs, have a long loop with a lead weight on the bottom and hook over the branch. I make the candles from carnauba wax, which makes them very hard, and I save my candle ends and melt them down, and I have a lot of beeswax that I put in. They'll burn for two hours or more.

The gingerbreads are a tradition of mine that started as soon as the children were able to look at the tree. We made farm animals and parrots and corgis, of course. They helped me paint them with white icing, which takes a bit of artistry.

I did all the tree decoration. The children weren't supposed to see it until Christmas night. It was set up in the parlor because I could shut it away there. After Christmas dinner the sound of the music box playing was the signal that it was time. It was a great big old-fashioned one, with those prickly rollers, that belonged to my father's family. There were eight tunes, and the boys' favorite was "The British Grenadiers." The children would rush in and see the tree in the darkened parlor with the candles all alight and their eyes would open wide with wonder and excitement.

I 'M perfectly content. I have no other desires than to live right here with my dogs and my goats and my birds.

I think I've done a good job of life, but I have no message to give anyone. If I do have a philosophy, it is one best expressed by Henry David Thoreau: "If one advances confidently in the direction of his dreams, and endeavors to live the life which he has imagined, he will meet with a success unexpected in common hours." That is my credo. It is absolutely true. It is my whole life summed up.

Selected Bibliography

Titles are arranged chronologically by date of publication.

Pumpkin Moonshine. Written and illustrated by Tasha Tudor. New York: Oxford University Press, 1938.

Alexander the Gander. Written and illustrated by Tasha Tudor. New York: Oxford University Press, 1939.

The Country Fair. Written and illustrated by Tasha Tudor. New York: Oxford University Press, 1940.

Snow Before Christmas. Written and illustrated by Tasha Tudor. New York: Oxford University Press, 1941.

A Child's Garden of Verses by Robert Louis Stevenson. Illustrated by Tasha Tudor. New York: Oxford University Press, 1947.

The Dolls' House by Rumer Godden. Illustrated by Tasha Tudor. Garden City, NY: Georgian Webb Offset, 1947.

The Dolls' Christmas. Written and illustrated by Tasha Tudor. New York: Henry Z. Walck, 1950.

First Prayers. Illustrated by Tasha Tudor. New York: Oxford University Press, 1952.

Edgar Allen Crow. Written and illustrated by Tasha Tudor. New York: Oxford University Press, 1953.

A Is for Annabelle. Written and illustrated by Tasha Tudor. New York: Oxford University Press, 1954.

Around the Year. Written and illustrated by Tasha Tudor. New York: Henry Z. Walck, 1957.

Becky's Birthday. Written and illustrated by Tasha Tudor. New York: Viking, 1960.

Becky's Christmas. Written and illustrated by Tasha Tudor. New York: Viking, 1961.

Take Joy! The Tasha Tudor Christmas Book. Selected, edited, and illustrated by Tasha Tudor. New York: World, 1966.

Corgiville Fair. Written and illustrated by Tasha Tudor. New York: Thomas Y. Crowell, 1971.

The Night Before Christmas by Clement C. Moore. Illustrated by Tasha Tudor. Chicago: Rand McNally, 1975.

The Christmas Cat by Efner Tudor Holmes. Illustrated by Tasha Tudor. New York: Thomas Y. Crowell, 1976.

A Time to Keep. Written and illustrated by Tasha Tudor. Chicago: Rand McNally, 1977.

Tasha Tudor's Advent Calendar. Written and illustrated by Tasha Tudor. New York: Philomel, 1988.

A Brighter Garden. Selected poems by Emily Dickinson. Illustrated by Tasha Tudor. New York: Philomel, 1990.

SOURCES: *A wide assortment of Tasha Tudor's creations — calendars, Christmas cards, valentines, reprints of early miniature books made for her children, replicas of her sketch books, lithographs, paper dolls, and illustrated books — are available from The Jenny Wren Press, P.O. Box 505, Mooresville, Indiana 46158.*

Annotations

❦

Frontispiece: Tasha working in her "studio," the corner in the winter kitchen where she works with her paints and pastels on an old trestle table, holding her drawing board on her lap.

Page vi: Sketch of daughter Bethany at age fourteen, knitting. Collection of the artist.

Page 4: Tasha wearing a dress of her own design. The child's dress belonged to one of Tasha's relatives and dates from the 1890s.

Pages 6–7: The azalea garden in late May.

Page 8: Tasha's bedroom. The dress she is wearing, as well as the one being held, are both from the 1830s, with gigot or leg-of-mutton sleeves typical of that period.

Page 12: Dark rust-colored dress circa 1830 with a hand-embroidered pelerine from New York State. The day cap was worn by older women and servants.

Page 13: Pocket watch belonging to Tasha's paternal great-grandmother, and miniature of Tasha's maternal great-grandmother, who died in her twenties in childbirth. The dress and hair style are of the late 1830s.

Pages 14–15: The crab apple orchard with underplanting of daffodils and narcissus.

Pages 28–29: The "lower garden" in early June.

Page 31: One of Tasha's borders from *A Time to Keep*, comprised of wild roses, daisies, clover, grasses, wild

strawberries, fringe corydalis, club moss, and a leopard frog.

Pages 36–37: Corgiville. Watercolor and pencil. Collection of the artist. The model for Corgiville was Harrisville, New Hampshire, "but I took liberties with it."

Page 50: Tasha working a marionette of Captain Kutasoff Hedzoff made for a production of William Makepeace Thackeray's *Rose and the Ring*. Tasha and the girl are wearing English dresses from the 1870s "bustle" period.

Pages 52–53: Marionettes made for *The Rose and the Ring*. From left to right: Countess Gruffanuff, Betsinda, the Italian artist Lorenzo, the guest conductor Pasquale Fellini, and Count Hogginarmo.

Pages 60–61: The front porch, with potted geraniums, gardenias, and foxgloves, and Tasha's favorite Boston rocker.

Page 62: 1870s dresses from Tasha's collection. The girl holding the mirror is wearing a great-aunt's dress from Indiana.

Page 73: Sketch of ducks, a rooster, and daughter Bethany drawing. Collection of the artist.

Page 77: The loom room where Tasha does her weaving, with Winslow Homer hat from 1860 and Regency-period birdcage.

Page 84: 1850s child's dress and straw hat, and pull toy

from around 1900. The background portrait is of Tasha's great-grandmother, who married Frederic Tudor, "The Ice King," when she was eighteen and he was fifty, and subsequently had six children. "She was furious; she thought she was going to be an old man's darling."

Page 89: Tasha's Peking robins, also called Chinese nightingales.

Page 87: Deer-footed mice. Watercolor and pencil. Collection of the artist.

Page 88: Barn tools, circa 1850. Hay forks, grain shovel, sap yoke, and a cheese basket for draining whey.

Page 103: Braided onions and chalk drawings on the wall next to the telephone.

Page 105: The kitchen, with copper hand pump, dried flowers, and nineteenth-century English lusterware china.

Pages 106–107: The "winter kitchen" fireplace, after a design by Count Rumford, which Tasha uses for cooking as well as warmth. Tasha's dress dates from the Civil War.

Page 111: Painted sled, made in Brattleboro, Vermont, circa 1860.

Pages 114–115: Painting done for 1988 Advent calendar published by Philomel books. Watercolor, ink, and pencil. Collection of the artist.

Pages 116–119: Tasha's dolls and dollhouse. Captain Thaddeaus Crane was made in 1953, and Emma Birdwhistle in 1980. The dolls are one-fifth life size.

Pages 126–127: Tasha at her stove, a "Canopy Grand" made in the early 1900s in Pennsylvania. Tasha is wearing her "parrot corsage," Hannah.